## Our Amazing Senses

# Our Skin Can Touch

by Jodi Wheeler-Toppen

CAPSTONE PRESS
a capstone imprint

Little Pebble is published by Capstone Press,
1710 Roe Crest Drive, North Mankato, Minnesota 56003
www.mycapstone.com

**Library of Congress Cataloging-in-Publication Data**
Names: Wheeler-Toppen, Jodi, author.
Title: Our skin can touch / by Jodi Wheeler-Toppen.
Description: North Mankato, Minnesota : Capstone, [2018] | Series: Our amazing senses | Audience: Age 4-7. | Audience: K to grade 3. | Includes bibliographical references and index.
Identifiers: LCCN 2017005231 (print) | LCCN 2017006589 (ebook)
ISBN 9781515767152 (library binding)
ISBN 9781515767206 (paperback)
ISBN 9781515767251 (eBook PDF)
Subjects: LCSH: Touch—Juvenile literature. | Skin—Juvenile literature. | Senses and sensation—Juvenile literature.
Classification: LCC QP451 .W44 2018 (print) | LCC QP451 (ebook) | DDC 612.8/8—dc23
LC record available at https://lccn.loc.gov/2017005231

**Editorial Credits**
Abby Colich, editor; Juliette Peters, designer; Wanda Winch, media researcher; Tori Abraham, production specialist

**Photo Credits**
Dreamstime: Maximillian100, 13; iStockphoto: kali9, 11; Shutterstock: agsandrew, motion design element, Anna Jurkovska, 17, Gundam_Ai, 7, Photographee.eu, 21, pixelheadphoto digitalskillet, 15, sciencepics, 9, Soloviova Liudmyla, 5, Tuzemka, 1, wavebreakmedia, cover, Yuganov Konstantin, 19

# Table of Contents

# A Soft Dog

**Woof!** Pet a dog.

He is warm. He is soft.

Your skin lets you feel.

# In Your Skin

Tap your chin.

Your skin has cells.

They feel the tap.

The cells send a signal.

It goes to your brain.

It knows the touch.

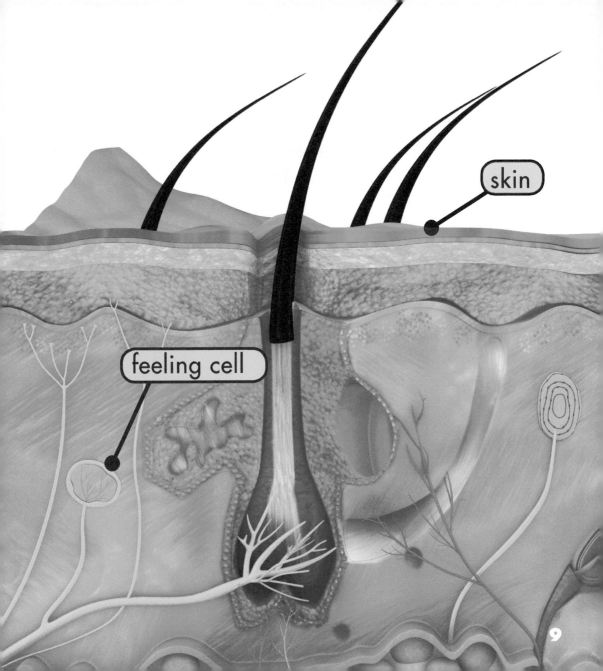

skin

feeling cell

Fingers can feel the most.

Lips can too.

They have the most cells
that feel.

# What You Feel

Uh oh! It's a bug bite.

Skin feels the itch.

Don't scratch!

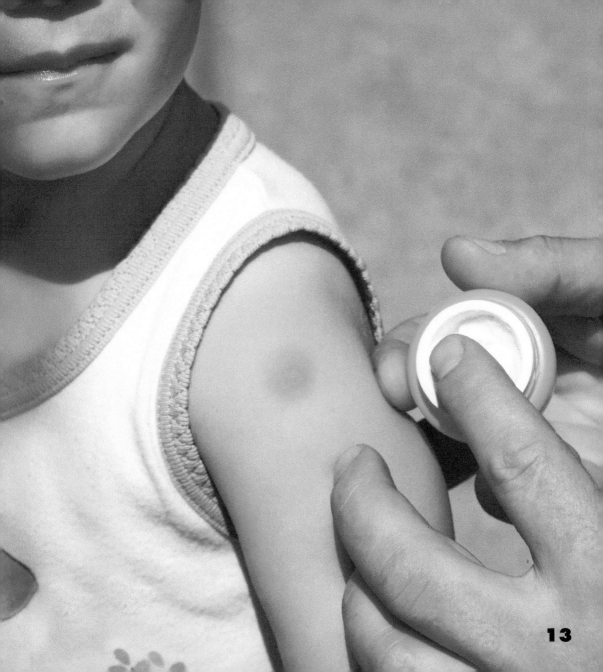

13

Give a big hug.

Hold on tight.

Skin can feel pressure.

Touch a rock.

Is it smooth?

Or is it rough?

Skin can feel texture.

You play in the snow. **Brrr!**
Then you sip
a warm drink. **Ahh!**
Skin can feel cold
and hot.

Oops! You step on a toy.

**Ow!** Your skin feels pain.

Move your foot now!

Touch keeps you safe.

# Glossary

brain—the organ inside your head that controls your movements, thoughts, and feelings

cell—the smallest unit of a living thing

pressure—the force produced by pushing on something

signal—a message between the brain and the senses

texture—the way something feels

# Read More

Appleby, Alex. *What I Touch.* My Five Senses. New York: Gareth Stevens Publishing, 2015.

Murray, Julie. *I Can Touch.* Senses. Minneapolis, Minn.: Abdo Kids, 2016.

Rustad, Martha E.H. *Touching.* Senses in My World. Minneapolis, Minn.: Bullfrog Books, 2015.

# Internet Sites

Use FactHound to find Internet sites related to this book.

Visit *www.facthound.com*
Type in this code: 9781515767152

Check out projects, games and lots more at
**www.capstonekids.com**

# Critical Thinking Questions

1. Name one thing that skin feels.

2. What two spots on your body can feel the most?

3. Reread page 20. Think of another way touch keeps you safe.

# Index